The Motherboard:
Key to Soul Prosperity

Freshwater Press

USA

All Scriptures taken from the KV of the Holy Bible, unless otherwise indicated.

Freshwater Press

USA

The Motherboard: Key to Soul Prosperity

Dr. Marlene Miles

ISBN: 978-1-960150-15-8
Paperback Version

Copyright 2023 by Dr. Marlene Miles

All rights reserved. No part of this book may be reproduced, distributed, or transmitted by any means or in any means including photocopying, recording or other electronic or mechanical methods without prior written permission of the publisher except in the case of brief publications or critical reviews.

.

Contents

The Motherboard 5

Celebrating Mothers & the Motherboard 10

    Motherboard 12

    A Soul 16

    Memory 17

    Survival Memory 25

Children 28

The *Evolved* Memory 35

    Keep Your Mind 37

Focus 43

    Know Your Emotions 48

Manage Your Emotions 51

Motivate Yourself 53

Recognize Emotions in Others 55

Worry 57

Give It Back 62

Conquer Worry 65

Order 72

Opportunities 74

Altar Call 83

Christian books by this author: 86

The Motherboard

Mothers--, the reason they praise so hard is because they've been through the *most*. The Mothers in the church have been through it all, they've seen it all. They've had heartaches, lonely nights, worry, worrisome children, husbands who won't do right or serve God, but will serve a lot of other stuff in the streets. Children in the streets. Sleepless nights. Deadlines without knowing how to meet them. Jobs that don't pay enough, or at all. Jobs they had to work to feed their families. Some mothers have had *me-too moments* all their lives, before and after they were Mothers. They weren't always old as you see them now, they've been beautiful, slim and trim, vibrant.

Now, they show signs of having lived the life that was presented to them. They have calloused knees for the right reason--, hours in prayer to the Lord and Savior of their lives, and for the lives of all that they have interceded for, for decades.

The hair on God's head is as white as wool; God is the Ancient of Days. So many Mothers, whether they go to the hair salon or not, they've got hair on their head like God--, white as snow. These moms know some stuff because they've seen some stuff.

Someone once said you don't get to be old by being ignorant. Mothers have had experiences that they've had to deal with wisely. No matter if you think Moms are smart or not, they are smart. No matter if you think they remember their youth and their lives or not, **they remember** – even if they are forgiving of the foolishness that you did and do because they are Mothers, or grandmothers. They are forgiving--, but they remember.

Like God.

Young people: Don't discount old people, they are the reason, many times that God didn't **smite** you when He could have or maybe should have. It was that praying Mother, or grandmother that stood in the gap for you. Don't discount them as old, or ancient because that's not an insult, since God is also the Ancient of Days.

Finally, when you get some years on you, hopefully you'll get to be more like God, too, when Wisdom is walking alongside you – like God, when you can finally say that Wisdom is your sister – which means that Wisdom, too, is no spring chicken.

Young people, you don't remember when you were five and your role models were all teenagers because you thought they were cool or fun, or maybe you thought they were smart. When you got to be a teenager you thought *you* were smart, too. All teenagers think that. They think they've got life all figured out and they really don't need to go to school or read books anymore. Some don't want to go to college, except to party and have fun.

Without having accessed Wisdom, especially in your youth, there are many 30, 40- and 50-year-olds still trying to hide or fix the stuff they did in their teens or twenties. Youth can be the most dangerous time of life for many. Not so much because you don't know much, but it's because you don't know much, but you think you know everything.

That is why you have parents.

And later, that is why God gives us Mothers to teach us what to do and what ***not*** to do based on knowledge, Wisdom and especially experience.

Foundational Scriptures

He who has my commandments and keepeth them. He that loves me, and he that loveth me
shall be loved of my father. And I will love him, and I will manifest myself to him. And I will manifest myself to him.

> John 14:21 NKJV

Beloved, I wish above all things you may prosper and be in health even as your soul prospers.

> 3 John 2, NKJV

Celebrating Mothers & the Motherboard

If you are in a church with a Mother Board and you have godly, patient Mothers, be thankful. Be grateful. Some people don't age as well as others; some can be bitter. We won't talk so much about bitter people in this book, nor do we recommend you stand in their counsel or sit in their company. Do not ever be disrespectful to an elder, but do not take their advice unless it is established by two or three and especially by the Word of God.

A church Mother Board is there to help us make right decisions and have right responses when life throws us curve balls. Mothers share with us and teach us from

Wisdom, understanding, knowledge, and most of all from experience. God gave us the church Motherboard. God gave us mothers, and you can't beat God at anything.

This book celebrates mothers *and* the Mother Board. It celebrates all people who have walked in the office of *Mother*, at any time, aunts, cousins, other relatives, friends and even strangers that God may have sent along the way. Those who fulfill the role of Mother have not always been the natural or birth mother, or even women.

This is not to offend, but sometimes *men* have served in that capacity. We appreciate and celebrate you as well, but you can't beat God. So, God gives us mothers, and He gives us a Motherboard. *Next, we celebrate our internal motherboard, which is the processor of information.*

Motherboard

The Processor of Information

Looking at the word, *motherboard* I realized that is what computer experts have created in **computers**. The thing that processes the information that comes into a computer is called a *motherboard*.

In your own life, when you have information that needs sorting or processing, this is when you invite Wisdom to walk alongside you. This is when you want to call Wisdom your Sister, your confidante and most trusted adviser. Since this book is really about the *motherboard* that processes all the information that **we** receive in our *own* computers--, **not** the electronic devices that we carry around or perch on our desks at work and in our home offices, or balance on our laps, but the information that we receive in **our mind, our brains**, in our persons. We will discuss how that *motherboard* works, and how to work it properly and to advantage.

You have a motherboard *on board,* we all do. That doesn't mean that we don't love and cherish the church's Motherboard and our own mothers, but we have a God-given *motherboard* on board, it is our powerful mind. It processes all of the information that we get from the outside.

The computer motherboard is based on ***our mind***.

There are 100 billion neurons in the human brain, each having about 15,000 connections. Your mind is dynamic and fearfully and wonderfully made. A computer is modeled after the human brain, except we are organic, and alive, while a computer is made of inanimate hardware. We have real intelligence; the computer is artificial intelligence, even though it boasts up to 65535 connections on one single IP address you still can't beat God.

With our natural minds, God has given us the ability to receive a lot of information, process that information and make right responses to the information received based on understanding, knowledge, Wisdom, and experience. We have experiences and *memory*, proving that we can learn, we can remember and learn again, become intuitive and wise.

Unlike a computer where information comes and is stored exactly as it comes in, *our motherboard* is subject to our experiences. It is subject to what we've been through in life. It's subject to how we see things. It's subject to how we have come to conclusions and reached summaries about things. So, when information comes in, it's processed through *our motherboard* that we have on board, it's colored by our experiences and personalities confirming that we are **human and not AI.** The human brain is efficient but 10 million times slower than a computer, operating on 12 watts of power; the average computer uses 175 watts.

God has given us this awesome way to process information. We have the ability for thoughts, ideas, and concepts to come into our mind, a way to nurture them and bring them up. In a sense, we have all *mothered thoughts*. We've all mothered ideas and inspirations where they may have come in small and then we grew them to big, wonderful things, to the glory of God. Or to our disappointment, we may have mothered bad ideas and harvested crops that we are ashamed of.

A Soul

I wish above all things that you may prosper and be in health even as your soul prospers. 3 John 2

We know that God regenerates us and gives us a new spirit when we accept Him, but what of our souls?

What is a soul? A soul is comprised of a mind, a will and emotions. Therefore, to prosper our souls, we must prosper *all parts* of our soul. We want to prosper or mature the mind, the will and the emotions.

Primarily, in this book, we will talk about prospering in our **emotions** although we may mention other parts of the soul.

Memory

Depending on what we have on board, I am sure that at some time or other, we could have grown ideas and thoughts into some things we may not like. We are personally responsible based on what we have allowed to come into our minds, and what we do with it once it comes in. The ideas, feelings, emotions, and impulses we receive can either be rejected or accepted. The impulses we accept are mothered to fullness. This mothering is based on who we are as a result of past experiences that we've either enjoyed or suffered.

Computer memory is how much space is left to cram some more stuff in it.

Whereas our memory is the stuff we already have in there, how it makes us feel, and how we *feel* about it. Our memory causes information and inputs to be subject to us. By this modality, God has given us memory, authority and responsibility over our actions, reactions, and responses.

There are all kinds of memories. There are flesh memories, such as when you hear a song that you used to hear in the world, you start tapping your foot and sometimes you can do the exact dance that you used to do in the world before you were saved.

I say *before* you were saved because people now-a-days believe they can mix anything and everything. No. Worldliness is not pleasing to God. Those who are friends with the world are enemies of God. You may argue that you need to be cool to fit in with people and co-workers. No.

When your *"undercover evangelism"* is **so good** that we can't tell who the sinner is and who is doing the work of the evangelist, then something is really wrong. Women especially, get from *under* those *covers* if you are supposed to be witnessing to a fellow and not wet nursing him.

If you don't let the Holy Spirit check you, you'll keep doing exactly what you've always done--, or worse. Doing the same dance moves as you did in the world is definitely because of flesh memory. The music is in your mind, in your memory. You hear it, and you just do the same thing that you used to do. You may have a soul tie with that song, or a soul tie with that time in your life. You may have a soul tie with the dance, or you may have made a dance covenant and not even be aware of it.

Yes, a *dance covenant*, as you are dancing, moving your body to that song you are AGREEING with the words of that song and anything subliminal that has been *programmed* into that song.

What difference does it make? A lot. Are the words declaring things such as you don't need any money, just your boo? Are the words saying that you'd gladly sleep with someone else's spouse for just one night? Those are covenants, which means sooner or later that sin, or a loss will present to you--, not fast enough for you to tie the things together, because you are *"just dancing"* or *just singing*, that's why I'm telling you, so you can either avoid it or at least recognize it when it comes. Worse, the opportunity to sin may not come fast enough to even get to you, it may be presented to your children, or grandchildren.

Once you're aware that an evil covenant exists, all of us can pray prayers to get out of evil covenants, but it will be up to you to **STAY** out of them. It is best to never enter into evil covenants, especially since it's difficult to know that you've entered into one if you've been deceived. The devil is tricky and tricks people often, too often, actually.

Singing is praying. Speaking is praying. Talking is praying. Singing is praying to music. Whatever the words are to the song *is* what you are praying--, over and over. **Do you realize that you've probably PRAYED the words to your favorite song, to the top of your lungs.** *AND* danced to it for 5, 10, 20 or more YEARS? Don't you pretty much *have* what you've been saying and praying all your life?

Depending on the words to "your song" or any other songs that you've been *praying* ever since you learned to sing, determines **who** you've been praying to. Godly words--, you're praying to God. Ungodly, secular, lustful, ridiculous words – those words all have gone to the devil's ears, and by so doing, you have authorized the devil by having created evil covenants–, mostly unknowingly. For years, the devil's been working hard to fulfill the disasters that you've spoken and **prayed** throughout your life, into your life.

Until you apply something new, until you apply the Word of God and the Holy Spirit you will keep repeating things because of flesh memories, which some call muscle memory. Soul memories are real and cause repetition in life as do COVENANTS, and agreements that you have made. Hopefully these covenants were made exclusively with God. Careful, the devil tricks folks into covenants to gain legal and I'll say, *semi*-legal access into your life all the time, all from **memories**.

Other flesh memories may come from childhood memories. Memories of the holidays may predominate; Momma was cooking, and you remember the smells through the house. Those flesh memories are imprinted in your mind, on *your motherboard*.

Even your hair has memory.

Beauticians, barbers and stylists can attest, your hair has memory. If you wear it curly long enough, your hair will behave as if it's curly and you can't get it to lay down straight, at all. Or if you wear it straight long enough it may not hold a curl till you get around the block.

Men, don't laugh. That's why some men wear doo-rags at night, so they can *remind* their hair to lay down, look wavy all the next day. Memory.

Flesh memories cause folks to have **addictions**. Because of fond memories of things that happen in and to our flesh we want to keep repeating it. Often, we are attached to things, stuff – food, beverage, events, music. Have you ever started humming a song that you couldn't get out of your head? Craving foods.? There's a thin line here because it depends on **_why_** you are behaving a certain way, whether it's a flesh or soulish memory, or both. But soulish memories are imprinted on the emotions. They cause us to have soul ties and be addicted to *people.* If we have relationships that we may have had to give up, but we didn't want to, we keep thinking on them or wanting to repeat them.

This book addresses emotional memories and how emotional, survival memories are pretty much alarmist and exciting. *Alarm* memories tell you that you need to take quick or drastic action, you need to *do something*. There's a threat, a disaster looming that you need to handle. That's survival memory. It's different than the casual fond, reminiscing, daydreaming type of memory.

Then there's an **evolved memory**--, it is the memory of the renewed man, the memory of the new man, the memory of the new man in Christ. **It's a whole different focus**. It's God-focused memory.

Survival Memory

Ultimately God gives us memory for our good; not to torment us. The devil misuses memory, if he can, to get into your mind, to torment and worry folk. God gave us memory for at least one very simple reason: Man has a tendency to forget. Well, at least we are better than dogs, whose memory is about 2 minutes, chimps 20 seconds, bees, 2.5 seconds and goldfish one month and a dolphin 20 years – I have my theories....

In man, initially memory was for survival. When men were living in caves and nomadic, memories were for survival so a man could remember that fire burns, ice freezes, fingers turn blue in the cold, and the last guy that ate the purple polka dotted berry died. Don't do that! Memory is for survival.

Survival memory is an emotional memory--, memories of *I want, I feel, I need, and* trauma memories. The stuff that's in your memory that kept you out of trouble or got you out of trouble is **survival memory**. The more intense whatever you went through, the more it's impressed on you, the more it will be impressed into you and affects your *motherboard,* the more it will affect your thinking and how you process things.

I am telling you all this because 3 John 2 says, *Beloved, that I wish above all things that you may prosper and be in health even as your soul prospers.*
Your mind, your emotions are part of your soul. I will tell you how to prosper your soul in this book.

Looking at our motherboards that we have on board, when we evaluate the impressions, imprints, thoughts that are in our mind, we will see that our overall memory is based on stuff that we have gone through--, a lot of it from infant and childhood years.

Mothers and fathers, the stuff you've done both *for* and *to* your children--, they haven't forgotten it. They may not have had words then to put it into a sentence and describe it to you or anybody else, but it's *impressed* in them. It's part of what makes them who they are, now and in the future.

Children

Children are not just little bundles of fun that you can throw into the air-- *and drop.* You can't do that. You have to treat children like the little souls, the little people that they are. God has entrusted you to treat them with respect and care. You can't treat them carelessly, thinking they'll forget it, or they won't tell. **It will all be told in the future, in how they handle themselves and live their lives.**

Children are real souls, real people. They have real impressions, real feelings, real hearts, and they remember things, although they may not be able to write it down in a letter to you.

Yet.

They may not be able to say it in any way other than crying, yelling, screaming or gibberish.

Yet.

But they remember and what happens to them makes an impression in their memory, in their souls. It causes them to react and respond the way they do when older.

Their memories cause them to be who they are, just the same as yours do. So we all live our lives based on memories **until Jesus comes in**, regenerates the spirit and renews the mind. But until that time for any of us, adults or children, we are conducting our lives on survival emotions. Remember that your child is a real person who has memories, some of them intense. For those who never get saved, they may be living their entire lives on survival emotions.

Have you ever noticed some gifted children or young people who may have so many gifts and talents and skills? Even people in your family? You wonder, why didn't that kid grow up and make something of himself, or why didn't she, go to college and make something of herself?

Aside from devilish and witchcraft manipulation, it's primarily because of the **emotional** part of the person. It's because of being in a place where their emotions needed to be controlled, but not just controlled – a person can only ***act*** but for so long. Those emotions needed to be renewed, disciplined, or washed by the water of the Word and restored. Not being able to control our emotions may hinder the success, and the prosperity that God has for all of us.

Children who go through a lot of emotional (survival) trauma as small ones, studies have shown that as they grow older, these are the children that are more prone to flunking out of school. These are the children who are more prone to getting into crime, drugs, and alcohol as if they are still in survival mode. Their childhoods could have felt like survival mode from the first day they got here. They had to have *survival emotions* because perhaps their needs were not met.

You may be one of those children yourself. You may have been one of those children.

Parents, I'm not beating up on you. To almost any child, or a childish, unsaved person, traumas and perceived traumas are tragic and dramatic because the devil is telling that soul to **overreact**. There's the devil perpetuating the trauma because the devil loves trauma; he uses it to get into people's lives, into their brains.

So a child will take any hurt or perceived hurt as far as he can. For example, a child tries to stand, he falls on his bottom. He screams bloody murder! He fell 5 inches onto a padded and carpeted floor, while his bottom is also thickly padded. It didn't hurt, but how do we know what his "mind" is telling him just happened to him. And we know this baby does not have the mind of Christ, he does not have a prospered soul. Yet.

Until Salvation and renewal of the mind, any of us, all of us might overreact because the devil is whispering to us. As a parent, you ask your child not to cry because it didn't hurt. And once the child realizes that it really didn't hurt, don't they stop crying, and they try to stand again?

So there's a survival memory, and we thank God for that because He put it in there to keep us alive and save our lives. But we should prosper our souls, getting out of survival living, by Salvation in Christ Jesus and submission to the work of the Holy Spirit in our lives.

Yes, God gave us memory, but it is up to us in our Christian walk to allow the Lord to renew our minds, renewing, re-focusing our memory and prospering our souls. As new creations in Christ, our memories now have the right focus. They have a God-focus and not the focus of impending doom, disaster, problems, or survival. In this scenario, even in everyday or dramatic situations we don't overreact; **this is soul prosperity.**

To the positive, when you're at work, for example, and there's a problem, but you're reacting in a completely different way than everybody else, because you're moving in soul prosperity.

As you prosper in your soul then God can bless you.

It is our job to cause our souls to prosper. When I mention survival memories do you think I'm talking about cave people? Nope. I'm talking about any of us. Because we have strong memories of stuff that happened to us, from childhood up to now. A lot of it you may not even be able to put into words because it may be things that happened to you as an infant or as a child before you could even talk.

You only know you flash back to a critical time when you felt a strong alarm inside yourself at an intense moment. When something like that presents again, you may react as a child again, because of that previous experience. This cycle may repeat until you get renewed by the regeneration of your spirit, the Word of God and/or the Holy Spirit.

I am a dentist. This phenomenon of which I speak happens to someone almost daily in my dental chair, or in some other dental chair across the world. I see and hear so many patients flashing back to when they were 5, 9, 10, 12 and even up to 16 years old. Some *older* patients recalling last month's extraction with the Oral Surgeon. PLEASE: if you are an emotional person, or dentistry triggers you, don't do this to yourself (or the dentist); get sedation dentistry until you get Jesus on board to change how your motherboard processes events and life.

The *Evolved* Memory

There's also what I call an *evolved memory*, the memory that Saved folk should have. It's the memory of the renewed mind. In survival mode, there's constant fear, distress, and threat. But when we become renewed, new creatures in Christ, we have a sense of security because God chose us, because God loves us. Because He's planning to keep us, and He does keep us, and He gives us comfort and allows us to dwell in safety.

In peaceful conditions we can renew our minds; in war, you cannot. If you're stressed, with constant fears of devastation, you cannot renew your mind. God gives us comforts so our souls can prosper. When our souls prosper, then the rest of our being can prosper--, our health and finances can also prosper.

If you look back at the temptations of Jesus, you'll see that they were all for *things and stuff.* Once Jesus made the right responses, He ultimately **received** the things and stuff. The focus was not to receive the things and stuff, the material gain, the goal was to pass the temptations, and model that success for us, which Jesus did. Jesus prospered in His soul, and we are supposed to be doing the same.

Keep Your Mind

Reviewing, God gave us memory so we could survive, learn, socialize, keep our minds stayed on Him **and** prosper in our souls. That's what memory and the renewed mind is supposed to do. When your mind is stayed on God, then your soul will prosper.

In the Old Testament the Israelites built memorials every time God presented to them in a new way. Every time He revealed a new aspect of His character. Every time God revealed a new attribute, He had them to build a memorial so they would remember that God is *this*, but He's also *this*. God is also *this*, *this,* and *this*.

We see that God has installed a brain with a memory and recall, a motherboard in man, and that's now how we build our memorials now.

God would say something to them such as, **Build a memorial here so you don't forget this. Not only so you don't forget, but also so you can tell your children and your children's children.**

Note that as the Israelites, were coming out of Egypt, they didn't build a memorial to remember how the Egyptians were cruel to them in slavery; that's the wrong focus. They built that memorial to remember that God delivered them out of the hands of Egyptian slave masters and multiple evil idol *gods*.

The memorials are now *inside* us because we are under the Better Blood and we're under the New Covenant. **As we build memorials in the mind, they should all be of Jehovah God**. This is how your soul prospers. Every memorial in your mind should be to and of God. Now how can that be? How can we do that? Let's see.

If you fall, or someone pushes you and you break your leg and it really hurts, how can your mind be stayed on God? If you're thinking about the person who pushed you and caused your injury? See how that's focusing on others. And the pain is also designed to make you flesh-focused.

Let's say if you broke your leg, you remember that Billy Boy pushed you and that caused the injury. So now you hate Billy Boy, but now that makes you Billy Boyfocused or other-focused.

You could be self-focused, me-focused. You could say, *Oh I knew my leg was broken right away and I went to the doctor and it's a good thing I was smart, and I knew it was broken.* That's me-Focused.

Or you can remember the time that **God** was your Healer, and your leg was broken, but He healed you and took the pain away. This is how you prosper in your soul. We can have situation after situation, but it is how we look at it, how we remember it, how we memorialize it, how we celebrate and recognize God that allows Him to manifest to us, and it also allows us to get to know Him even better because we all have plenty of opportunities to get to know Him.

Your focus needs to be on God. Now that you're healed, you come into a testimony service and you say what a good job the doctors did and you forget that **God** is the one that healed you, though the average doctor will gladly take credit. You still haven't prospered in your **soul** because you have not given God what is due Him. **You prosper in your soul by keeping your focus on God.** So if your perspective is not on God, if it's not right, then you will keep going through things.

Jacob's spotted, speckled, and ringstraked cattle multiplied after their own kind, and especially after what they looked at. Keep your mind stayed on God.

Keep your eyes on God. Faith comes by hearing: keep your ears on God so your life will look more like God and less like Billy Boy and even less like _yourself_.

In John 14:21God says He wants to reveal Himself to you. He wants to manifest Himself to you. And when you recognize God in a situation, especially a crisis, you _get it_, and your soul prospers. It's not a one and done, it is progressive soul growth to full maturity.

So that's why you're going _through_, because every time you go through something in the natural, it's a reflection of what's happening in the spirit. Once you _get_ what God is trying to show you, once you recognize that it's God, then you can pass to the next test. If you don't recognize, acknowledge God, and give Him His props, you will keep _going through_ until you do acknowledge Him--, meet Him.

It's how you look at things that confirms that your on-board _motherboard_ is working, and how it's working. It's how you look at things that tells you if you're looking at it from God's point of view or from a people point of view, or from a selfish, me-point-of-view, exclaiming, *"Look! I did all of this great stuff myself!"*

God-focused, this is how your soul prospers. No other person has the ability to prosper your soul. No other entity has that ability.

Focus

If you have a memory of when you met God, that's God-focused. But if you have a memory of *all that you went through* and how terrible your life was leading up to the point that you met God, but you don't mention God, that's not God-focused; that's self-focused or problem-focused.

We want our souls to prosper. We need our souls to prosper; it is a mandate. If you have a memory of what God has done for you instead of how **you** pulled yourself up by your bootstraps, that's God-focused. How **you** did it is **me**-focused. Soul prosperity is always the goal.

Without the Spirit of God, YOU in and of yourself have no ability to prosper your soul – you can only stay the same, if you're lucky. Mostly, in the world we live in you will default to rust, decay and deterioration; we live in the Earth, where things can rot and rust.

You might argue that you have *willpower.* Sure, you do. But will power to change into **WHAT**? If you don't see GOD, there is no way to aspire to be more *godly*. If you don't hear God, if you don't feel GOD – there is nothing to aspire to. You will start to look like what you see, feel, and hear. Flesh, and worldliness.

Every memory that you have should be of how you saw **God** – high and lifted up. How you heard GOD, and His voice was like thunder upon the waters--, many waters. How you felt GOD in your being, in your body when He healed you, it was like fire! How you felt Him in your soul; so, you know that GOD is real. Every memory should be of when God did something for you--, how

God *delivered* you and then how **God** blessed you, how **God** kept you, how God saved you. How God provided for you in each one of those memories in one of His attributes that is new to you, in a new character of God that you had not seen before.

Its God, your Healer, God is your Provider. God, your Protector. God, your Keeper. God is your Helper. This is soul prosperity.

Each of those memories are memorials. They are memorials to remind you of how awesome God is.

Normal people don't erect memorials for bad things. And how many people do you know who go out to war, lose the war, then come home and build a monument because they *lost* the war. I'm not talking about propaganda where a war was lost but people-built memorials to all the losing generals to convince themselves that they did well, like so many kids playing stick ball and everyone gets a trophy, even the nonathletic kids.

Memories of negative, losing events --, you don't put stones for that. You don't put up those roadblocks. You don't put up those bad things if you have a renewed mind. Memorials of *what happened to me,* how bad it was, or I was so beautiful then.

So you don't do it in your mind either. We are aspiring to soul prosperity.

Even the times when God disciplines you--, **I was going the wrong way --** He disciplined me, and I was able to turn back to the right way. That's soul prosperity.

God gives us a way. He gives us so many ways to reach Him and to grow, to develop, and bring glory to His name.

Memory directly affects emotions--, very profoundly. Memory of what we've been through, what we experienced, how it felt, how uncomfortable it was or how great it was, causes us to respond a certain way when the same thing, or something similar happens again. It causes us to respond either the same way or completely the opposite way if we feel we didn't respond the right way when it happened the first time. We may respond another way because **we remembered** what already happened.

Memory, a crucial part of our motherboard.

God gives us memory on purpose because He needs us to remember things. **What God really wants us to remember is *Him*.**

Know Your Emotions

To have soul prosperity you need to study and show yourself approved.

First, study yourself: Know your own emotions. You need to know your own emotions. Recognize your own emotions. Even if they're ugly. Because how are you going to deal with emotions that you don't recognize or cannot *name*? You need to recognize your own emotions even if they're ugly and deal accordingly. If not, you will be at the mercy of your emotions.

In managing your emotions, learn what emotions you're prone to. You know, for instance, if you're worried or if you get sad or depressed, you need to know yourself and so you can then learn to manage your emotional states better so you can prosper in your soul.

If you don't recognize what emotion you're having, it'll run all over you and have you doing all kinds of things. And it puts you back in that survival mode. **Survival mode** will be like an alarm going off, like, oh, there's a threat or there's a danger or something getting ready to happen. *I have to do something. I have to take action*. And then you take a drastic action for something small.

Know your own emotions. That's your job. You can't expect anyone else to explain your emotions to you. You'd be pretty offended if they tried. I know a man who tried to tell me how I was feeling--, often. That didn't work out well--, at all.

Ugly feelings and emotions may cause you to act ugly; that is not soul prosperity. Recognize your own emotions, because if you don't, you may have a tendency to be an alarmist –you may overreact.

Now that you're bigger, older, have more influence and more ability, you might *really* overreact--, just because you *can*. Survival emotions are **NOT** God's plan for our lives.

Manage Your Emotions

You need to be able to manage your own emotions. Be self-aware. If you're upset, you need to be able to calm yourself down.
That's your job.

Find center again. Quickly.

You need to know how to, and be able to shake it off and move on to the next thing, whether it's gloom or anxiety, irritability, whatever it is. *Beloved, prosper in your soul*; your soul needs to be resilient, another marker of soul prosperity.

Have your emotions, express yourself (without sinning), but it is the resilient man who can be blessed of God and used by God.

Motivate Yourself

You need to know how to motivate yourself. David encouraged himself in the Lord. You also need to know how to encourage yourself. If you can't think of anything else, then think of what God has already done for you, and that'll encourage you. Open your Bible and find out what God says about you. That will encourage you and this is how you prosper your soul.

Motivate yourself. Encourage yourself. You need to know how to chill out when it's time to chill, and how to encourage yourself when it's time to take action. You especially need to keep your flesh under because your flesh can slow you down considerably. It also can provoke you to do things that you will wish you hadn't done, later on.

The flesh can be very unpredictable.

Keep your flesh under. That's how you manage emotions. Especially if you have a tendency to open your mouth and tell people *a thing or two.* Keep your flesh under.

Speak words of encouragement over yourself*: I am the righteousness of God in Christ Jesus. I am blessed coming in and blessed going out. Yeah. I'm just gonna go out just to be going out to see if I'm blessed, then I'm gonna come back in because God said it, it must be so. Thank you, Jesus.*

Recognize Emotions in Others

Empathy is recognizing emotions in others.

You want to be a soul winner? You want to witness to people? You don't **tell** people how they are feeling, you ask them. This is a people skill.

You want to be a soul winner? Then use your spiritual gifts. A word of knowledge or a Word of Wisdom is huge in locating people where they are and being able to minister to them. The world calls it a people skill. being able to talk to people.

For this book the final mark of soul prosperity is evidenced in how you handle your relationships.

Summarizing: Know and manage your emotions, encourage yourself, recognize emotions in others, and handle relationships. This is by no means the whole list of how to prosper in your soul, but it will get you off to a great start.

Worry

For instance, if you are a worrier, you need to know something about worry. Get some books on it, study on it, look in the Bible, of course, and find out what God says about it. Find out how to handle worry. Yield to the Holy Spirit so He can do a work in you.

Worry is playing a little soap opera over and over in your head..., and you're the star. Thinking *What if* all day long? *What if? What if? What if?* all day. Then when you get through thinking, *What if?* for that particular day, then you go to the next part: *Then what if?*

You've got on your cape or whatever you chose to wear in this little video you've got going around in your mind and you are thinking, *what if* this happened to this person? Or what if this happened to me? Or *what if* this situation arose? Or what if the check didn't come or what if it didn't get deposited in the bank? And you're thinking, what am I going to do if that happens, while trying to figure out how to avoid a problem. That's the plot of soap operas, telenovelas, they are all melodramatic and you're the star.

What if my child stays out too late? What if there's a fire? What if there's an accident?
What if, what if...,

So we worry and worry, then when the thing we were worried about, **doesn't** happen, we think we **helped** it to not happen by worrying. We feel rewarded because it *didn't* happen because we think we **helped** it not to happen.

Then, as the soap opera turns, some of us don't even turn the channel. We go back to worrying about some other aspect of the same thing over and over, and we keep worrying and worrying. *Then, what if... then what if...., then what if.*

When that **next** thing doesn't happen, we really think we helped. We didn't help anything at all.

Or some of us when we worry, we feel guilty that we *caused* it to happen--, by worrying.

Folks, if we have this much power to *cause* things to happen and to cause things to **not** happen by *thinking* about them, we should be living in some serious victory. If you know that you have a power to *cause* things to happen, why would you think on things that you don't want to happen?

As a man thinketh, so is he.
Proverbs 23:7a

Not as a man *thinketh*, so is the world, or his world around him, just that man. So, your worrying doesn't affect anyone but yourself.

>A man can have whatever he says.
>(Mark 11:23)

Now, when the mouth is engaged things become more dangerous. Depends on your faith. Who you are to God, how much spiritual authority you have.

So, there you were practicing all of these potential disasters in your mind. Worrying, all day long and half the night.

>Therefore I tell you, do not worry about your life, what you will eat or
>drink; or about your body, what you will wear. Is not life more than food, and the body more than clothes? ... Can any one of you by worrying add a single hour to your life ?
>
>Matthew 6:25 and 27

In all your worrying can you turn one gray hair black? No, but you surely can turn black hair gray. The Word says not to worry or be anxious for anything.

Believing in the *power* of your worry -if you are so powerful to be able to *cause* things to happen, why does it take *all day* or all week worrying? If we have this ability, through worry – which is UNGODLY, then why does it take **so much worry** to make things happen, or stop things from happening? Why can't we worry for 10 minutes and make it happen or *not* happen?

Because **worrying is NOT doing what you think it is doing. It is making things worse, far worse and the <u>worst</u>.**

Give It Back

Give your worries over to God, or in most of our cases, give what you are worrying about *back* to God because He probably had it in the first place. Then you impatiently said something to God like, *"Give me that. You're not working on it fast enough. You're not doing it right. Give me this. I want to worry about it some more."*

Since you're a child of God, whatever you're thinking on, is God's--, His car, His house, His child, His mortgage payment. It's God's *everything*, we've just got stewardship. He can handle this situation. That's why you should let your motherboard kick in. Now we want to prosper in our souls, and God is giving us a way to do that. He's given us an escape, a way to solve real problems. He wants every thought in our motherboard, everything in our memory bank or in our brains to be of ***Him***. This deactivates the power of the enemy in our situations and empowers God to move on our behalf.

When our focus and perspective is right, whatever issue comes along we apply what we have already experienced, what we know and what we understand to it, we will make right, wise, renewed-Mind decisions and responses.

We won't act like people who don't have a God. We won't act like people who just don't know what's going to happen tomorrow. Because we have security, we're secure in Him. He gives us everything we need and more.

Church Motherboard, our real mothers, we love you, and we pray and believe that you will always give us good counsel based on Wisdom, understanding, and especially experience. And the motherboard, that we have on board, as long as we keep the right imprints in there, we also believe that all this wise counsel will line up with the Word of God.

We remember that we are not cave people, we are not unsaved people, and we're not animals. We are *highly evolved* creatures, created just a little lower than the angels, is what the Psalm says. We are living, moving, breathing beings; our souls should prosper. God gives us a soul that's just a small thing, think of it as a seed, that God tells us where to prosper it. And as we prosper it, God blesses us.

Conquer Worry

How do we conquer worry? Let your motherboards kick in. If you don't **challenge** worry, it gains like a snowball rolling downhill.

Scriptures tell us to cast down imaginations. When worry comes, we say, *"Wait a minute, wait a minute, that's exalting itself against the knowledge of God. I will not even think on that."*

You can think up some horrors, fires, floods and other crazy things. All that exalts itself against the knowledge of God because God promised He would keep me. *God promised He would give His angels charge over me to keep me in all my ways. He promised that I would be blessed coming in and going out.*

Study the Word of God, show yourself approved, get some Word in you to get over worry. Challenge worry; don't let it have its way, no matter how much you like being the star of the melodrama. No matter how much you like inserting YOURSELF in a person's life, in a place that has **nothing** to do with you. That's God's place to save them, keep them, not yours.

To overcome worry, you need to come up with a more pleasant scenario **that does <u>not</u> include you. Challenge worry** by saying, "God said He would keep me, so that's not gonna happen." Or, *God said that He would protect my child, so I have to take my hands off of this situation, because I'm not God.*

You say you trust God, but you don't trust your child, their friends, their ability to make wise choices, and you definitely don't trust the streets. You've got to trust that God is bigger than the streets and has authority over your loved one.

Trying to have God -focused thoughts and memory in a crisis is nearly impossible if that's not your day-to-day baseline. If you need one-another support and help, reach out for it. You don't have to go far, but if you need to, call a friend, someone you know who's really God-focused who can tell you where to look in your Bible. Call a Deacon or a minister. Call somebody if you have to.

Don't go down that spiral of worry. It's not worth it, and it's not soul prosperity.

Receiving the Word, you find that you can cast your cares on Him because He cares for you, and that you are to be anxious for nothing, and that He never sleeps or slumbers. Even if it's the middle of the night. Still, He's watching over your situation. His eye is on the sparrow, so you know that He's watching you and the situation or person that's worrying you.

Give it to God. He's never failed me. Get friends who appreciate the **real** you, so you don't have to make up a fantasy to save the world or save the day and be the superhero. That's not soul prosperity. You're important to somebody without heroics. Just be you.

New Creation, New Creature, New Mind

To be renewed, become a new creature, a new creation, you need a renewed mind too. That means you don't keep doing the same stuff you used to do and doing it the same way. Get saved, but that's not all you do. You know you're on the way to Heaven, yet you keep doing the same stuff you always did is not soul prosperity.

Your motherboard activates with the memories and imprints of what God did for you before. How God brought you through before, how the check did come in the mail, how it got deposited to your account. That the mortgage was met. That your child came home from the street, how God did it before, how He healed you before. How He delivered you, set you free. How He saved your people and your family? You just let that motherboard kick in with those memories that give you peace, solace and rest.

If the scenarios that you are picturing, thinking on, or worse, speaking on are NOT what God says then you are practicing demonic outcomes, negative, destructive, and ungodly outcomes, and you are practicing **witchcraft**—perhaps blindly, as a blind witch, but it is *witchcraft*.

God says He will supply all of your needs according to His riches in glory. As an example, we live in a natural world where we may need to go get firewood to make a fire in the hearth, but God said HE would supply. If you didn't take the time to ask God where to go get the firewood, when to go, who to ask, but instead relying on YOURSELF that's not what God said. Now the worry of a cold house, who will get sick, who will die because of this cold, is not unrealistic if it's really cold outside and there's no other heat source. But practicing the horror of it in your mind is not healthy. Especially, when a friend of yours already called and asked you, *Why don't you come and stay with me during this cold snap, we've got plenty of room and a back up generator.* God already provided; did you accept?

Order

The motherboard's got work to do in this situation. The motherboard has to come in and process all the information received. And, if a worry comes to your mind, the first thing you do is apply some Word to it. Cast down imaginations and every high thing that exalts itself against the knowledge of God.

Let's say, the check *didn't* come. Let the motherboard give you a reasonable situation you think on that. Don't worry about the negative things like that you think are you apply some word of God to it.

So what you do is cast your cares on Him. **So, at least if the situation is dire, real solutions are on this end of the thought process, not on the drama-disaster end of it.**

God is watching, He never sleeps and never slumbers as you walk upright before the Lord, not defiled. *(A nod to Mother Richardson): Just think on these things.* Think on those things that are lovely and true and have good report. This is what a seasoned, church Motherboard does for you. This is what a godly, nurturing mother does for you. This is what a God-focused thought life does for you. This is how your thought life needs to be to prosper, and this is how your emotions can prosper.

Then God can prosper you in other aspects of your life as well. Prospering in our souls is manifested in **order**. As we prosper, God shows up again. God keeps manifesting Himself with a new attribute in a new way with new character.

Opportunities

Don't think that nobody's been through what you've been through, that's not the case. Jesus went through a lot for us, to understand things that are common to men.

What you are going through maybe none of your friends have experienced, maybe no one in your family, but somebody, somewhere has.

Jesus has.

That is a devil-trick to keep people away from other people, to make you go into hiding, so he can continue to torment, ravage, hurt, steal from or even kill you. It is a trick of the devil to keep you from telling on him and getting help from others and the Lord. Don't believe the devil, ever. Don't believe it.

We have opportunities to be hurt, opportunities to overreact. Jesus certainly did. We have opportunities all of our lives to exhibit soul prosperity or its polar opposite.

Jesus was born and placed in a manger. What! Wait! A manger, in a barn? That would have been too much for most of us right there, even as newborns, looking around telling our parents with screams and cries that this is not good enough, this is not acceptable. Asking them, non-verbally, *Are you kidding me right now?* And then the judgmental, "*I didn't ask to be born.*"

Jesus was on the run, lied on, stolen from--, you name it. These things have probably happened to some of you too. But He kept His focus on God, which caused His **soul to prosper.**

What did you do when any of this happened to you?

By so doing, Jesus received spiritual authority, place, position, which is what we want. He stayed focused on God for a prosperous soul because he had a renewed mind, the Mind of Christ. A prospered soul has the Mind of Christ. *Let this mind be in you that was also in Christ Jesus.*

It's OK to have emotions. Jesus had emotions, He got angry, He wept. He went to celebrations. Humans are supposed to have emotions, but your emotions need to prosper.

If you are not in a survival state, there is no need to reacting with survival emotions.

Your emotions need to improve, period. It's like using your outside voice inside…. ALL the time.

Most likely when you were born, you weren't placed in a barn, in the animal's feeding trough. As a child, you probably had a lot of creature comforts and enjoyed being a child, so much so that when you're older, you're still childlike? If so, that's an indication sometimes that your emotions have not prospered. It could be an indication of witchcraft attack or evil exchange, but that's another book.

(See the book, **Blindsided: *Did the Old Man Bewitch You?***, by this author.)

One of the simplest and first steps to soul prosperity is forgiveness. Also developing in any and all of the Fruit of the Spirit leads to soul prosperity. Prayer, praise and worship help develop the Fruit of the
Spirit.

Reading, studying the Word, washing by the Water of the Word leads to soul prosperity. Practicing any of the Disciplines of the Faith will increase the maturity of your soul.

You can remember how your parents kicked you out of the house that is an opportunity to be traumatized, me-focused, hurt and defeated. But then your internal motherboard kicks in and you remember that when your mother and your father forsook you, the Lord took you up. That's soul prosperity.

Forgive them. That's another step to soul prosperity. Honor your father and mother, no matter what they did to you, yet another step into soul growth. God says that it will be well with you when you honor your parents, and God avenges all disobedience Himself. But God only avenges disobedience in *your* obedience. So don't act up.

You're always thinking of Billy Boy, Billy Boy, Billy Boy, what he did, what he said, or whatever. Aren't you tired of Billy Boy? I'm tired of Billy Boy *for* you. That's an opportunity to react against Billy Boy, but then your motherboard ignites the Fruit of the Spirit, and you *respond* to Billy Boy instead of reacting to his antics. Forgive Billy Boy, then forget about it. Be God-focused. Drop anything that will not prosper your soul.

Over-focusing on Billy Boy leads to idolatry. Vengeance against Billy Boy is for the immature and unprospered soul, and vengeance is demonic because you will not know how much payback is *enough* for Bill Boy embarrassing you on the playground in the 3rd grade. Vengeance is the Lord's; let it go.

Sure people have done stuff to me. I fear God's wrath toward them more than I fear anything *I* would ever do to them. Because I'm not going to do anything to a saint of God, or any person that God has told me not to *touch*. I'm pretty sure God has told them not to touch me (His child) too. Therefore they have something coming from God, perhaps for my sake, but **not from me**. Therefore, I can leave that right there, and so should you.

You need to let the Holy Spirit in there; be **_filled_** with the Holy Spirit because the Holy Spirit will bring the attention back to Jesus. Being Jesus-focused, God-focused will always prosper your soul. Your flesh may be pointing to one person if you're soul tied either thinking you're in love with that person, or you hate them. Your emotions will have you pointing at another person which is also not conducive to maturing your soul. But the Holy Spirit will direct your focus by pointing it to Jesus. *End*

Thank you for your time. Shalom.

Prayers

Beloved above all things, I wish you would prosper and be in health even as your soul prospers.

Lord, thank You for this word. Thank You for the *spirit* of it, as it goes into our very souls as it permeates into our minds, Lord, so we can have a new understanding of what soul prosperity is and that how important our soul is and how important it is that we prosper it not just for the living here, but so we can be well pleasing to You just as Jesus was.

Jesus made right, God-focused choices, decisions and responses and not just selfcentered or self-focused reactions. Thank You, Lord, that we have the Word of God, and that we can study, showing ourselves approved, rightly dividing that Word, Lord.

We thank You, Lord, for one another ministry. For where we don't have enough focus on You another saint will come and embrace us with the Word or embrace us with the Truth and embrace us and make sure we stay focused.

Lord God, thank you especially today for mothers who have kept so many of us focused that have prayed for us and who have loved us and have told us to keep our minds stayed on Christ because we know that You will not forsake us.

Lord, we thank You that through understanding and Wisdom, knowledge and even experience. Our memories will be more focused on you, our minds will be stayed on You, Lord. And because we trust You, You'll continue to bless us. Lord, we love You and we thank You. We praise You in the name of Jesus. Amen.

Altar Call

If there is anyone today who has read and understood this word, but you're not saved? You now know about the renewed mind and soul prosperity in Christ, and you want that? You have learned that Christians are different in their mind and their responses.

Are you one of those people who have not accepted Jesus Christ as your Lord and Savior, but you want your life to improve? To be different? Today, right now, you may come, today. He is calling for you to accept Him as the Lord and Savior of your life, to be forgiven of all sins and to receive Eternal and abundant life now here on Earth. You could be a new creation in Christ, and you can have the renewed mind and the soul prosperity of which we speak. Is there anyone?

Now believe in your heart and confess with your mouth that Jesus is the Son of God and that He died for your sins and on the third day God raised Him from the dead. Amen! Praise God.

Romans 10:9-10

Thank You!

The Motherboard: The Key to Soul Prosperity is the jumping off book for a soul prosperity collection of books.

Souls in Captivity
https://a.co/d/fnpviBh

Soul Prosperity: Your Health & Your Wealth
https://a.co/d/5oaPT9O

As My Soul Prospers
https://a.co/d/9xi2FYu

Christian books by this author:

AK: Adventures of the Agape Kid
AMONG SOME THIEVES

As My Soul Prospers

Behave

Churchzilla (The Wanna-Be Bride of Christ)

The Coco-So-So Correct Show

Demons Hate Questions

Devil Weapons: *Anger, Unforgiveness & Bitterness*

Do Not Orphan Your Seed

Do Not Work for Money

Don't Refuse Me Lord

The FAT Demons

got Money?

Let Me Have a Dollar's Worth

Living for the NOW of God

Lord, Help My Debt

Lose My Location

Made Perfect In Love

The Man Safari *(Really, I'm Just Looking)*

Marriage Ed., *Rules of Engagement & Marriage*

The Motherboard: *Key to Soul Prosperity*

Name Your Seed

Plantation Souls

The Poor Attitudes of Money

Power Money: Nine Times the Tithe

The Power of Wealth

Seasons of Grief

Seasons of War

SOULS in Captivity

Soul Prosperity: Your Health & Your Wealth

The *spirit* of Poverty

The Throne of Grace, *Courtroom Prayers*

Time Is of the Essence

Triangular Powers (4 book series)

Warfare Prayer Against Poverty

When the Devourer is Rebuked

The Wilderness Romance

Other Journals & Devotionals by this author:

The Cool of the Day – ***Journal***

got HEALING? Verses for Life

got HOPE? Verses for Life

got WISDOM? Verses for Life

got GRACE? Verses for Life

got JOY? Verses for Life

got PEACE? Verses for Life

got LOVE? Verses for Life

He Hears Us, Prayer Journal *4 colors*

I Have A Star, Dream Journal *kids, teen, young adult and up.*

I Have A Star, Guided Prayer Journal**,**

    J'ai une Etoile, Journal des Reves

    Let Her Dream, Dream Journal

    Men Shall Dream, Dream Journal,

    My Favorite Prayers (in 4 styles)

    My Sowing Journal (in three different colors)

    Tengo una Estrella, Diario de Sueños

<u>**Illustrated children's books by this author:**</u>

    Big Dog (8-book series)

    Do Not Say That to Me

    Every Apple

    Fluff the Clouds

    I Love You All Over the World

    Imma Dance

    The Jump Rope

    Kiss the Sun

The Masked Man

Not During a Pandemic

Push the Wind

Tangled Taffy

What If?

Wiggle, Wiggle; Giggle, Giggle

Worry About Yourself

You Did Not Say Goodbye to Me

www.ingramcontent.com/pod-product-compliance
Lightning Source LLC
Chambersburg PA
CBHW061338040426
42444CB00011B/2986